T0023467

The Call to Hajj

The Call to Hajj

Salwah Isaacs-Johaadien

Illustrated by
Karen Tuba

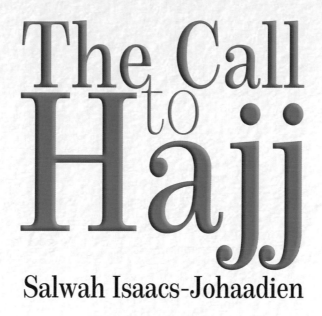

Published by Tughra Books
335 Clifton Ave.
Clifton, NJ, 07011, USA
www.tughrabooks.com

Library of Congress Cataloging-in-Publication Data

Names: Isaacs-Johaadien, Salwah, author. | Tuba, Karen, illustrator.
Title: The call to Hajj / Salwah Isaacs-Johaadien ; illustrated by Karen Tuba
Description: Clifton : Tughra Books, 2022. | Audience: Ages 7-9 | Audience: Grades 2-3
Identifiers: LCCN 2022001020 (print) | LCCN 2022001021 (ebook) | ISBN 9781597849487 (hardcover) | ISBN 9781597849821 (ebook)
Subjects: LCSH: Muslim pilgrims and pilgrimages--Saudi Arabia--Mecca--Juvenile literature. | Islamic stories--Juvenile literature. | Islam--Juvenile literature.
Classification: LCC BP187.3 .I735 2022 (print) | LCC BP187.3 (ebook) | DDC 297.3/52--dc23/eng/20220129
LC record available at https://lccn.loc.gov/2022001020
LC ebook record available at https://lccn.loc.gov/2022001021

Prophet Ibraheem, with Ismaeel, his son,
Was told to build the Kaa'bah in Bakkah.
Allah ordered, when the building was done,
That he call people to the Hajj in Makkah.

Prophet Ibraheem wondered how his voice would be heard
Across the mountains and desert sands.
"Call and they'll come," Allah reassured.
They'll answer from near and faraway lands.

2

Prophet Ibraheem always obeyed his Rabb.
Though puzzled, he did his best to do good.
The faithful man climbed a high mountaintop
And called out as loud as he could.

And true to the word of Allah Most High,
The call travelled to reach its aim.
From the earliest days and as time went by,
From all parts of the earth people came.

They came on foot, having no other means,
On a journey often many years long.
Trudging long, dusty roads and deep ravines,
Resting in towns as they went along.

They were not long distracted by changing scenes,
The faith in their hearts kept them strong.
Their goal was to answer the call of Prophet Ibraheem.
Round the Kaa'bah they'd call out in the throng:

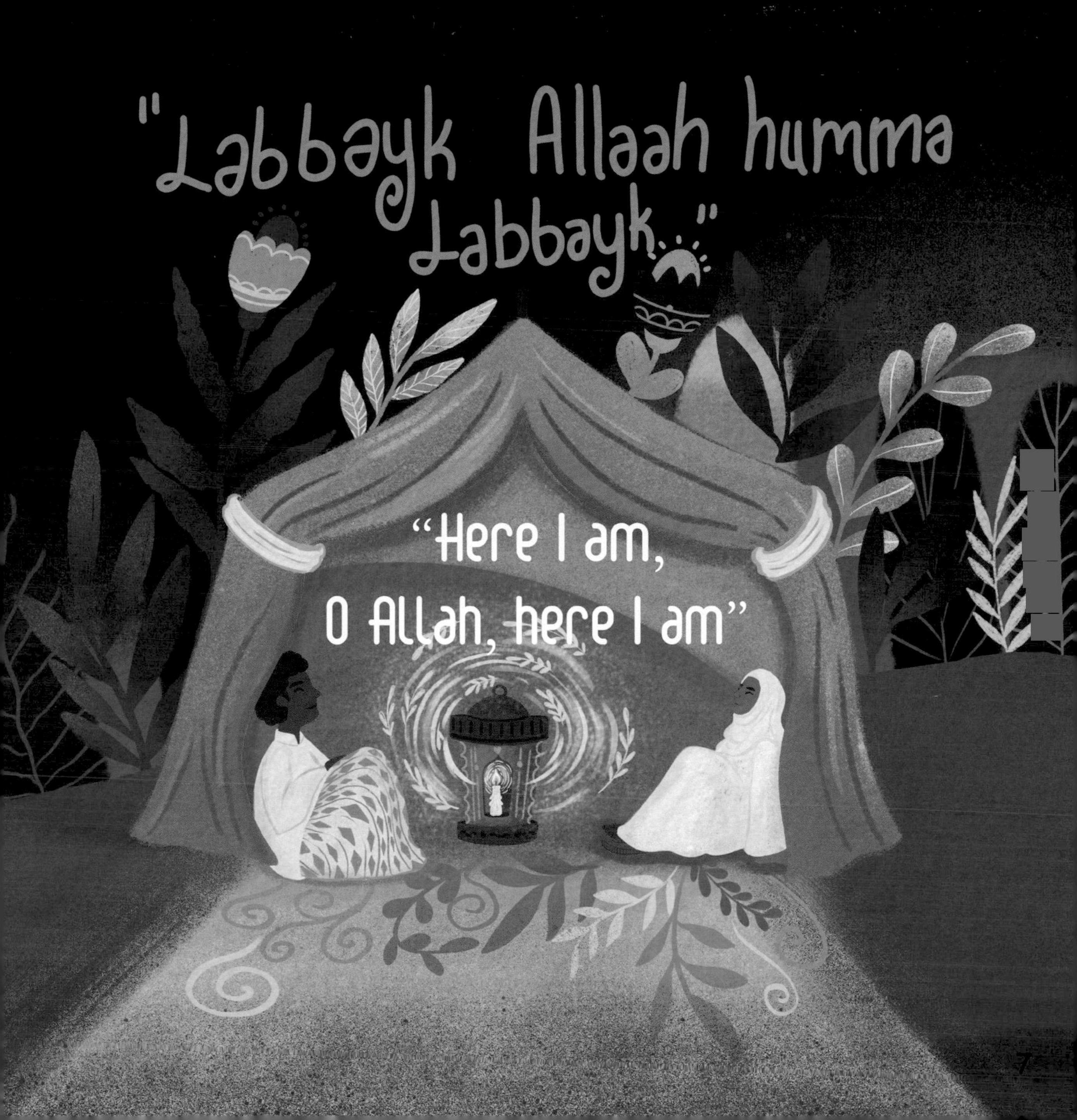

"Labbayk Allaah humma Labbayk..."

"Here I am, O Allah, here I am"

They came by horse, alone or together
Travelling for months on the road.
In rickety carts; on saddles of leather,
Clattering along paths wide and narrowed.

Steadfast they rode in all kinds of weather,
Passing markets and palaces that glowed.
They thanked Allah when their horses could tether.
Between Safa and Marwa their cries echoed:

Labbayk Allaah humma labbayk!

"Here I am,
O Allah, here I am"

11

They came by camel in a long, winding train,
Plodding for weeks through the desert.
Little to see across sandy terrain –
A rare Bedouin tribe or a lonely lizard.

Days of scorching sun and no drop of rain.
An oasis! Their prayers were answered.
They watered and rested, then pushed forward again,
To reach Mina where the pilgrims gathered.

Labbayk Allaah humma labbayk!

"Here I am, O Allah, here I am"

They came by dhow and ferry and ship;
    A tiny speck on the vast, open sea.
A journey of months, or a few days trip;
    From every distant and nearby country.

Winds, waves and pirates in times of hardship.
Breathtaking views when sailing was easy.
They crossed the seas to complete their worship,
To stand on Arafat, Mount of Mercy:

Labbayk Allaah humma labbayk!

"Here I am, O Allah, here I am"

They came with a steam train built for the Hajj,
That shortened the time of their travels.
Carriages crammed with people and baggage,
It took five days to work the coal shovels.

18

Through farmland and mountains – a scenic passage,
Through the desert, fearing Bedouin rebels.
Chugging along ridge, rattling over bridge,
At Muzdalifah they'd pick up pebbles.

"Labbayk 'Allaah humma Labbayk"

"Here I am,
O Allah, here I am"

They came by plane flying high in the sky.
Above the birds, cruising far up alone.
Through puffy clouds, a delight to the eye;
In turbulence a moan and a groan.

They ate and rested as the time flew by;
Just a few hours to cross a time zone.
They landed the same day they'd said goodbye;
At Mina they would pelt devils of stone.

Labbayk
Allaah humma labbayk!

"Here I am, O Allah,
here I am"

Year after year they completed the Hajj rites,
They sacrificed and shaved after pelting.
Then they returned to the Hajj holy sites,
for more rituals before departing.

On the days of Hajj they relived the life
Of Prophet Ibraheem and his blessed family.
The deeds of the prophet, his son and wife
Taught them to accept Allah's tests patiently.

Through the call to Hajj Allah invites us
To walk in the footsteps of Ibraheem (alayhi salaam).
To earn Allah's reward and forgiveness,
And fulfill the fifth pillar of Islam.

So as time goes by, we'll continue to come
from every place with all types of vehicle.
A high speed train or jumbo jet for some,
for others, a bus or a bicycle.

How will you answer the call to Hajj?